101 Creative PRAYER IDEAS

Eleanor King

kevin mayhew

kevin
mayhew

First published in Great Britain in 2018 by Kevin Mayhew Ltd
Buxhall, Stowmarket, Suffolk IP14 3BW
Tel: +44 (0) 1449 737978 Fax: +44 (0) 1449 737834
E-mail: info@kevinmayhew.com

www.kevinmayhew.com

9 8 7 6 5 4 3 2 1 0

ISBN 978 1 84867 945 0
Catalogue No. 1501571

Cover design by Rob Mortonson
© Images used under licence from Shutterstock Inc.
Typeset by Angela Selfe

Printed and bound in Great Britain

Contents

Sorry Prayers

Prayers for other people

Prayers for ourselves

Things to remind us to pray

About the Author

Eleanor lives by the seaside in Essex
with her husband and three children,
and buckets and spades on the doorstep.

She spends a lot of time running different groups
in the community, both inside and outside
the church, but when she is not doing this
she likes to make biscuits, go walking and
knit things that are not too big or complicated.

Introduction

Prayer doesn't always have to be about words. There are lots of ways that we can grow closer to God, using all our senses and doing things which we enjoy. This is true for all of us, but particularly true for children, who are often naturally active and busy. It is lovely for children to learn traditional prayers by heart, but as well as this, we can offer them opportunities to pray through making, doing, eating, drinking, playing, looking and exploring. And as we do this, we may well discover a fresh way for us to draw closer to God as well.

In this book the prayer ideas are grouped under different headings — thank-you prayers, sorry prayers, prayers for other people, prayers for ourselves, and things to remind us to pray. Among these there will be something for every occasion, whether you are looking for a quick activity to fill a few minutes, or a number of reflective activities on a theme to fill an afternoon. Many of the ideas can be adapted for large or small groups, and are suitable for different ages (suggestions for which ideas are most suitable for which age are included).

I hope you will enjoy these ideas and have as much fun using them as I did trying them out with my family.

Thank-you Prayers

Prayer 'lucky dip' bag

Get into the good habit of thankfulness with
this fun group prayer activity.

Fill a cloth bag with different objects that remind us
of things we can be thankful to God for – things like
pretend food, plastic animals, toy emergency vehicles,
a water bottle, a toy stethoscope etc.

The children sit in a circle and pass the bag around.
They can take out one item each from the bag in turn
and say a simple prayer (for example, 'Thank you, God,
for fire engines', or 'Dear God, thank you for sandwiches')
and everyone can join in with the 'Amen'.

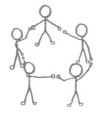

Age group: under 5, 5–7, 7–11

'Thank-you' lunch boxes

A lovely way to remember to thank God for our food.

Give everyone a plastic takeaway container with a lid —
either ones that have been washed and saved, or bought
(I have seen packs of eight in the pound shop).

Provide some permanent markers for children
to decorate the containers with the words
'Thank you, God, for our food' (or similar) and
add any pictures or patterns.

They can then take the containers home to use and
the decorated lids will be a reminder to be
thankful to God for the food that is inside.

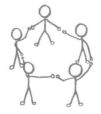

Age group: 5–7, 7–11

'Under the sea' mobile

Thanking God for the different creatures
and praying for their environment.

The frame can be made from sticks,
with cotton thread tied onto them and
cut-out creatures (for example, whale,
dolphin, starfish, octopus, fish, shark etc.)
suspended from that.

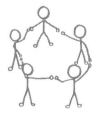

Age group: 5-7, 7-11

A cardboard treasure chest

A treasure chest to make and fill with plastic gems or cardboard gold coins, thinking about and being thankful for the real treasure that God gives us.

Empty fruit or herbal tea boxes make fantastic treasure chests as they are a good size and some have a lid that opens and shuts. It is also easy to make a treasure chest from an A4 piece of card, with equal-sized squares cut out from the corners, folded and stuck together with tape to make an open box shape. Coins can be circles cut from gold or silver card, or can be plastic milk bottle lids wrapped in foil.

Make a label for the box saying 'God's treasure' and children can label the coins with things that they are thankful to God for (for example, love, peace, family, safety, friends etc.). Younger children can either name things as they put the treasure into their chest, or could draw on the coins.

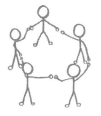

Age group: under 5, 5–7, 7–11

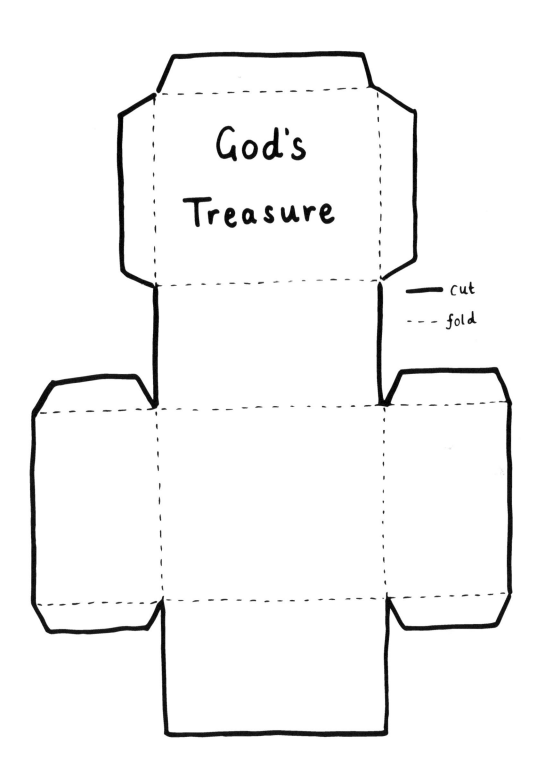

God's Treasure

cut

fold

Binoculars

To make and look through, to look out for the lovely things in God's world and decorate with a 'thank-you' prayer:

'Thank you, God, for your lovely world.
Help us to notice the beautiful things you have made. Amen.'

Young children can simply decorate the card with their favourite colours or some stickers. The binoculars can be made from half a piece of A4 card, cut in half and the sides rolled up to create two tubes. Secure the tubes with sticky tape and add a length of wool so that children can hang the binoculars round their neck.

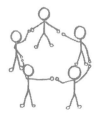

Age group: under 5, 5–7, 7–11

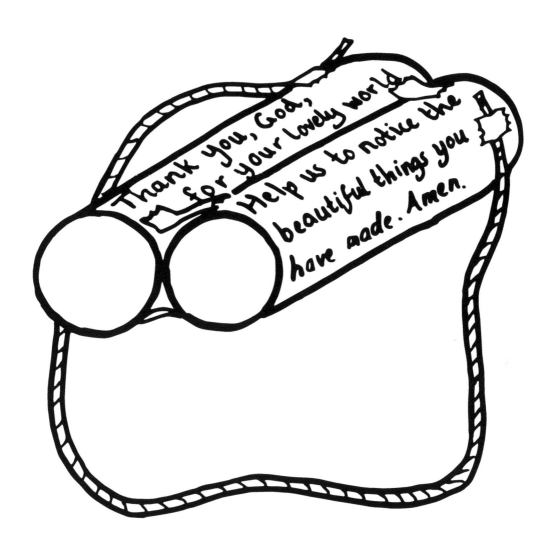

Pass the parcel prayers

When the music stops, unwrap a layer and read the prayer!

Children could write thank-you prayers on brightly coloured paper, wrap them up in groups, then swap parcels with another group. Younger children could just enjoy opening the pass the parcel, and have pictures of the lovely things God gives us in each layer (animals, food, sunshine, family etc.).

A budget way of wrapping pass the parcels is to alternate layers of newspaper with old paper bags. This makes it easy to see which layer is which, and afterwards they can be separated into two piles for recycling. Of course, groups of very young children will need paper for all the layers, to be safe.

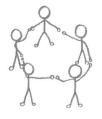

Age group: under 5, 5-7, 7-11

Stained glass window prayers

Get a large piece of flat clear plastic (perhaps from some packaging),
some glue and some tissue paper, crepe paper or coloured cellophane.

Everyone chooses a piece of paper and cuts it into
a shape of something to give thanks for.

This could be on a theme, for example,
Harvest Festival or Mothering Sunday.

The shapes can then be stuck onto the plastic
with the glue (overlapping is fine) to make
a colourful and bright prayer window.

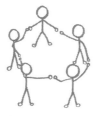

Age group: 5–7, 7–11

THANK YOU, GOD,

FOR THE HARVEST

8

Alphabet thank-you prayer

Sit in a circle and start with 'A', e.g.

'Thank you, God, for antelopes',
'Thank you, God, for antelopes and biscuits',
'Thank you, God, for antelopes, biscuits and crayons' . . .

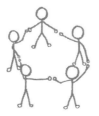

Age group: 5–7, 7–11

9

Prayer guitar

Make and decorate cardboard guitars,
with straps made of ribbon.

It works well to use cardboard tubes from the inside
of a roll of foil or wrapping paper, with the body of the
guitar cut out from card and stuck onto this.

Write on things like 'Praise God!'
'Sing to God', 'Sing praises' etc.

Put on a favourite hymn or song and the children
can all play along on their prayer guitars.

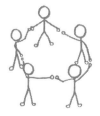

Age group: 5–7 7–11

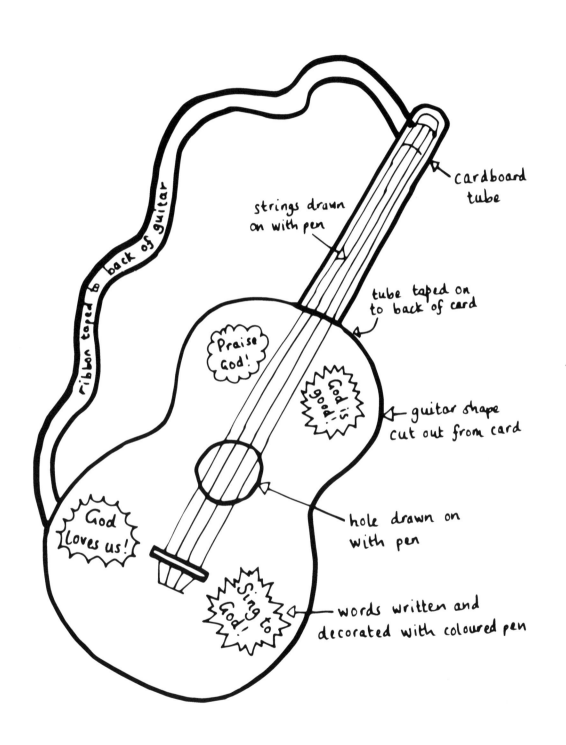

cardboard tube

strings drawn on with pen

ribbon taped to back of guitar

tube taped on to back of card

Praise God!

God is good!

guitar shape cut out from card

God Loves us!

Sing to God!

hole drawn on with pen

words written and decorated with coloured pen

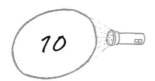

Prayers written on reflective or shiny paper

Use, for example, foil, wrapping paper or old gift bags
spread around a dark room. Children can have torches and
search for them. Words such as these could be used:

'Jesus, please bring your light and joy to people who are sad',
'Jesus, please bring your light and healing to people who are ill',
'Lord, please bring your light and peace to places where there is fighting',
'Lord, bring your light and love to people who are lonely',
'Lord, bring your light and wisdom to world leaders', and
'Jesus, bring your light and comfort to people who are worried'.

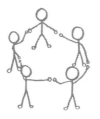

Age group: 5–7, 7–11

'Praise God' flicker book

Cut a piece of A4 paper into ten equal-sized pieces
and staple them together to make a small book.

Starting with the last page, write the words
'Praise God!' in bubble writing and colour them in.
Work your way back through the book, using the page
behind to trace from, leaving out another letter each time.
The first page will have just one letter on it.

As you flick through the book, the words 'Praise God!' will appear.

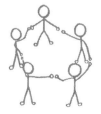

Age group: 7-11

Favourite animals

Make favourite animals out of modelling clay,
pipe cleaners or something similar.

Put them on a fabric landscape, with a sign saying
'Thank you, God, for all the animals'.

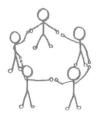

Age group: under 5, 5–7

Thank you, God, for all the animals

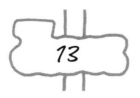

Decorated names

Decorate names of Jesus/names of God
(e.g. Saviour, Son of God, Bread of Life, Redeemer,
Good Shepherd, Lamb of God) by writing them in
bubble writing, colouring them in and cutting them out.

Tape or staple the words onto a long ribbon,
which can be hung up with a loop tied at the top.

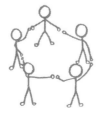

Age group: 7-11

card stapled to ribbon

Decorated plates and cups

Decorate paper plates and cups with the words
'Thank you, God, for inviting us to your party'.

Have juice, crisps and biscuits and join in God's party together.
Talk about how we are all part of God's family and
he wants us to celebrate that together with him.

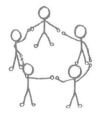

Age group: under 5, 5–7

Cocktail umbrellas

Place cocktail umbrellas on play dough islands, labelled
'You are our shelter from the storm, and our shade from the scorching sun'
or the words 'God looks after us' for younger children.

Talk about how we can come to God when
we are sad or worried and he will look after us.

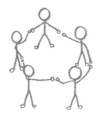

Age group: under 5, 5–7

16

Toothbrushes

Get cheap toothbrushes
(the supermarket or pound shops are good for these)
and decorate them with marker pens, saying:

'Thank you, God, for clean water'.

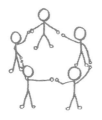

Age group: 5-7, 7-11

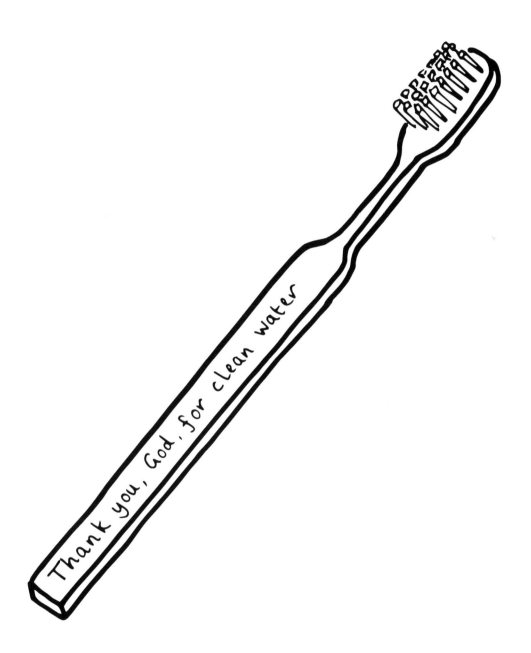

Praise collage

Photocopy and enlarge some favourite hymns, perhaps from an old hymn book.

Give the photocopies to the children to cut out words from and make into a collage of praise.

They can arrange the words of praise on a colourful piece of paper and stick them down with glue.

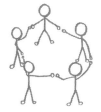

Age group: 7-11

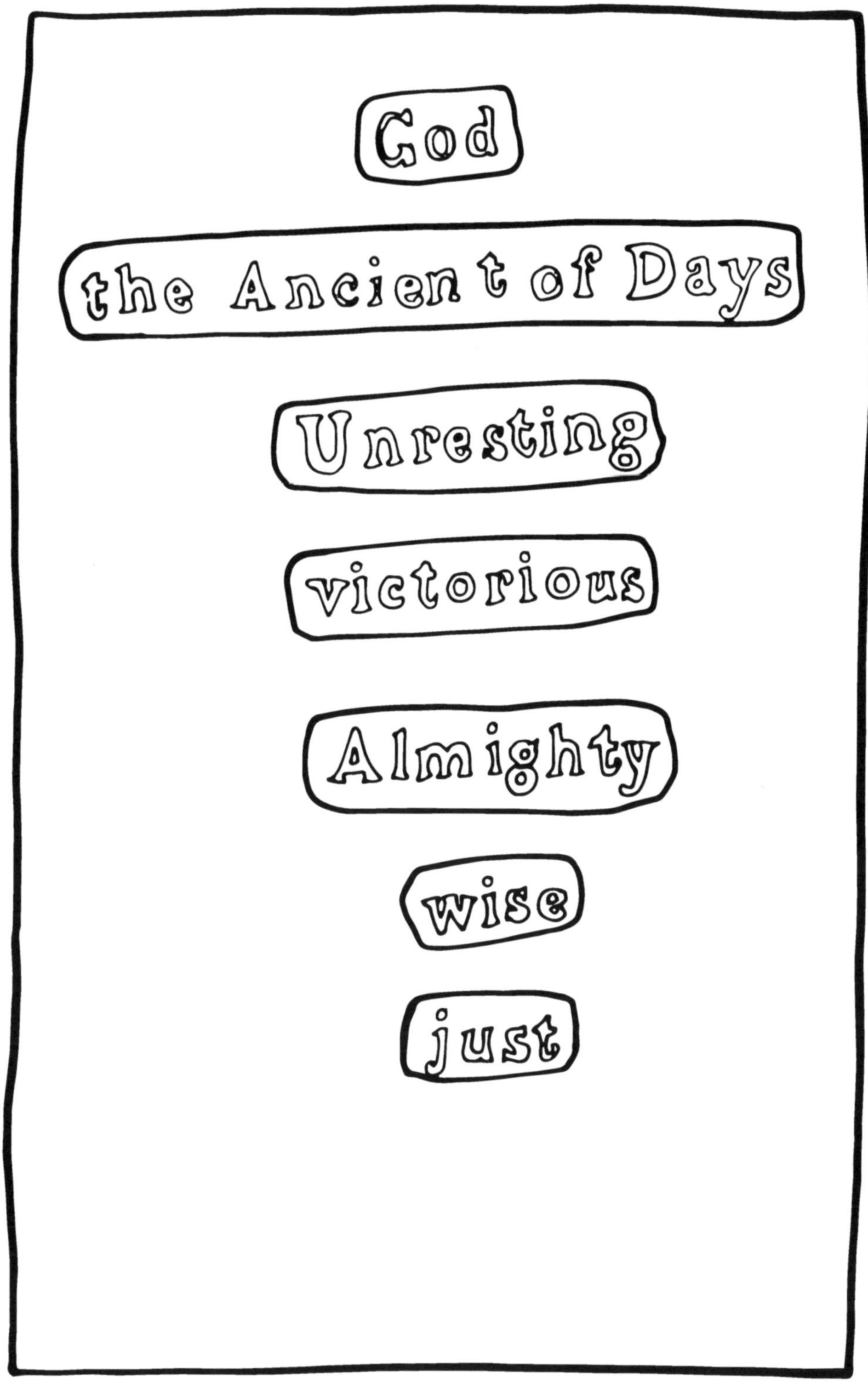

God

the Ancient of Days

Unresting

victorious

Almighty

wise

just

Paper napkin prayers

Write a short prayer on paper napkins with a ballpoint pen
(this is waterproof and also doesn't leak into porous paper)
thanking God for our food. For example,

'Dear God,
When it's breakfast, lunch, dinner or tea
I give thanks for the food
you give to me.
Amen.'

Children can also decorate the napkins
with pictures of their favourite foods.

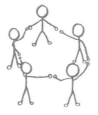

Age group: 5–7, 7–11

Dear God,
when it's breakfast, lunch,
dinner or tea,
I give thanks for the food
You give to me.
Amen.

Feathers

To think about God's gentleness give everybody
a feather to hold during a quiet circle time,
perhaps with gentle music on in the background.

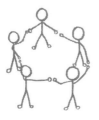

Age group: under 5, 5-7, 7-11

Raisin boxes

Label raisin boxes with the words
'Taste the sweetness of God's love'.

Younger children could cut out and glue on a square of paper
that already has the words printed or written on it.

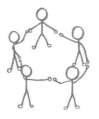

Age group: under 5, 5–7, 7–11

Hen and chicks

Make a cardboard hen with chicks hiding under her wing
(use a split pin to make the wing move).

The words 'Lord, you shelter us under your wings'
can be written on the wings of the hen.

Talk about how God loves us and cares for us
like a hen looks after her little chicks.

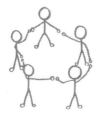

Age group: 5-7, 7-11

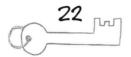

Key ring

Make and decorate a key ring in a key shape with the words
'You open up heaven to us, Jesus'.

The tags can be made out of paper or card,
coloured in, then laminated and a hole punched
in them so that they can be attached to a key ring.

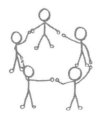

Age group: 5–7, 7–11

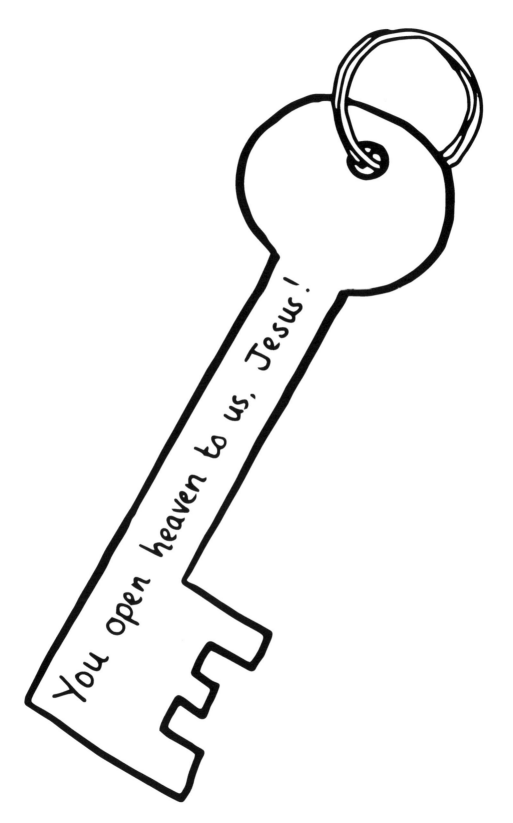

You open heaven to us, Jesus!

Fuzzy felt thank-you prayers

Cut out the words 'Thank you, God' from felt
(the children can help if the outline of the letters is drawn on first).

Next give the children a plain piece of felt and some scissors each,
and maybe some templates of animals, dinosaurs, fruit,
people, trees etc. if you have them.

Ask them to think about something they are thankful for and
to cut it out. (It doesn't matter if it doesn't look exactly right —
God knows what they are thinking.)

The youngest children could play with several pre-cut felt shapes.
A carpet tile works as a large fuzzy felt base to assemble
the felt 'thank yous'.

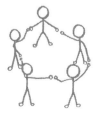

Age group: under 5, 5–7

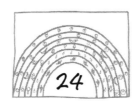

Big rainbow thank-you prayers

Draw the outline of a rainbow on a large piece of card or paper.
Colour the end of each band with the right colour
(red at the top, then orange, yellow, green, blue and purple)
so that children know which is which.

Stick pictures of things we are thankful for on the different colours
(e.g. strawberries and tomatoes on red, foxes and
clementines on orange, sunshine and bananas on yellow).

These could either be things that the children draw
themselves on blank paper, stickers, or things cut out
of catalogues and magazines.

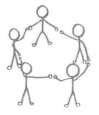

Age group: under 5, 5-7

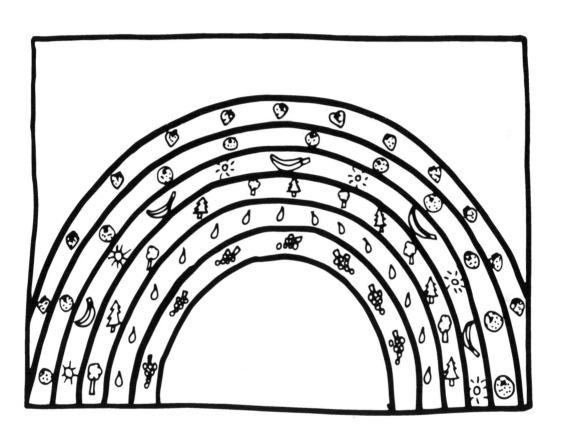

Nature 'lucky dip' bag

Pass the bag around the circle.
Everyone says something to describe the object
and then thank God together for his lovely creation.

It might include a feather, stick, pine cone, acorn,
leaf, sheep's wool, shell, stone, lavender or a flower,
or any other natural objects.

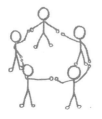

Age group: under 5, 5-7, 7-11

Prayer flags

Write and decorate words of praise on triangles
of fabric with permanent markers or crayons,
sew them onto a long piece of bias binding
(or tape them onto a piece of string)
and hang it up to display.

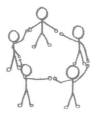

Age group: under 5, 5-7, 7-11

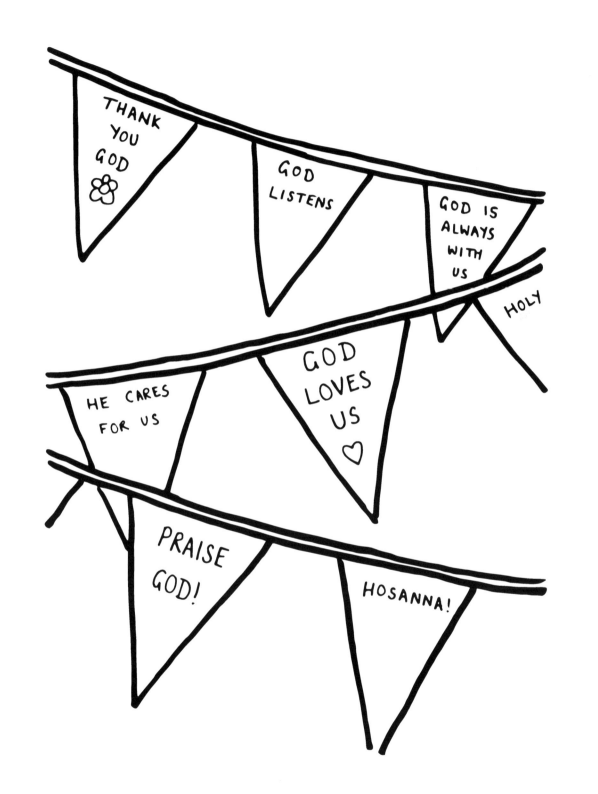

27

Prayer phrases

Prepare strips of card with prayer phrases on,
for children to choose, assemble and stick onto card
and add words of their own.

They could choose 'Dear God', 'Dear Jesus', 'Lord',
or 'Father God' to start their prayer,
then choose any combination of
'thank you for . . . ',
'please help . . . ',
or 'sorry about . . . '
and then finish with an 'Amen' card.

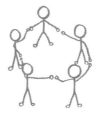

Age group: 5–7, 7–11

DEAR GOD

THANK YOU FOR

Chocolate

PLEASE HELP

All the refugees

SORRY ABOUT

Annoying my brother in the car

AMEN

Potato printing

Use biscuit cutters to make different symbols —
cross, dove, heart, candle, star.

Put a prayer at each table for people to read, while they add the
symbol to their paper, making patterns if they would like to.

Cross — 'Jesus, we know you understand what it is like to be in pain or feel
sad. Thank you for being with us when are in pain or feel sad too.'

Dove — 'Dear Lord, please bring peace where there are arguments,
whether they are big or small.'

Heart — 'Thank you, Lord, for your love for us.
Please fill our heart with love for others too.'

Candle — 'Dear Lord, please help us to shine brightly in the world
and light up other people's lives too.'

Star — 'As the wise men followed the star to find you, Jesus,
help us to notice the signs that you are here with us too.'

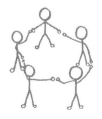

Age group: under 5, 5-7, 7-11

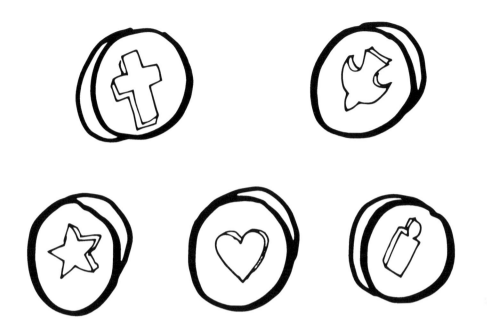

Sorry Prayers

Forgiveness flags

Wash away the things which cause unhappiness
and see God's message of forgiveness and love.

You will need some squares of plain fabric (a few different
colours if possible), washable pens, permanent markers,
clothes pegs, a washing line and a bowl of water.

Give everyone a square of fabric and ask them to write something on the
fabric that needs God's forgiveness, using the washable pens. These can be
general examples, such as being jealous, hitting, saying unkind things etc.
Children can decorate the word in colours that they think look miserable.

Now, put away the washable pens and ask people to write
the words 'God Forgives' in permanent marker on top.
They can add some bright, happy colours as well.

Once everyone has done this, they can take their fabric to the
bowl of water and wash it. The washable pen will disappear,
leaving the bright colours of the permanent marker and the words
'God Forgives'. After people have squeezed out any extra water,
they can fix their flags on the washing line, using the clothes pegs.

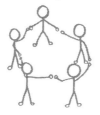

Age group: 5–7, 7–11

1.

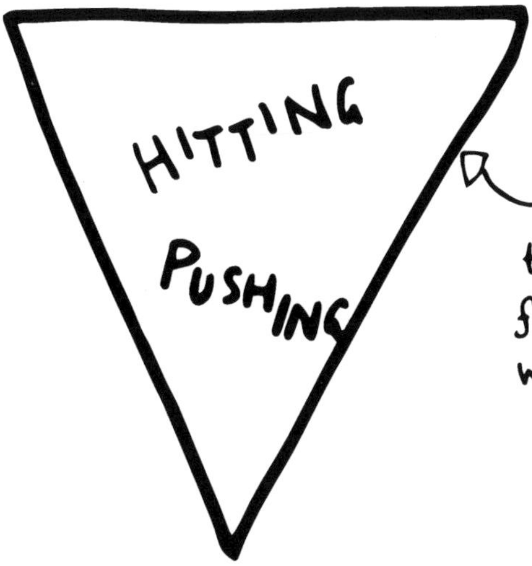

HITTING

PUSHING

— Write words of things which need forgiving in washable pen.

2.

~~HITTING~~ GOD

FORGIVES ~~PUSHING~~

— Write the words 'God Forgives' in colourful permanent marker.

3.

△ Wash fabric flag in water

GOD

FORGIVES

— The words 'God forgives' stay on the fabric!

Bubble wrap sorry prayers

Everyone has a square of bubble wrap and sits in a circle.

The leader says:
'For the times we've been selfish/hurt others/said unkind things/
been jealous/not looked after the world around us . . .'
and everyone replies 'Sorry, God', and pops a bubble,
to show that those things have now been forgiven.

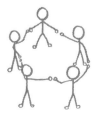

Age group: under 5, 5-7, 7-11

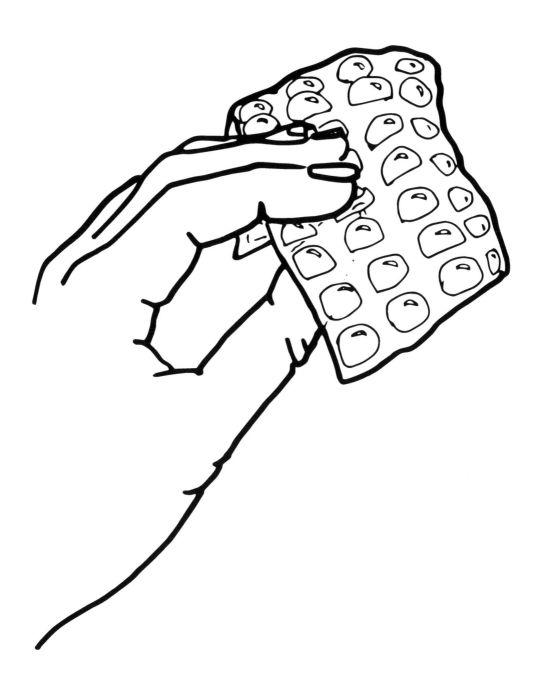

31

Shadow puppets

Cut out two cardboard shadow puppets
(just a simple outline of a person is fine).

Hang up a sheet or drape one over a table, with a light behind it.

The children can take it in turns to put on a show in pairs,
where the two characters have some sort of argument
or conflict and then make peace with each other.

Younger children could be supported by adults to use their puppets
and given ideas about what they could be talking about
(for example, 'I think the puppets both want the same toy').

Talk about how God forgives our sins and he also
wants us to forgive other people too.

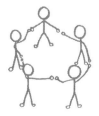

Age group: under 5, 5-7, 7-11

A group muddle

Children hold hands in a muddle as a group.
If they simply hold any other random two hands
of people in the group, this will make a lovely knot!

Another child untangles them, helping them see how to climb
over or under other people's arms until they are in a circle
(sometimes this game ends up with two circles, but this is fine too).

Explain that God helps untangle us from our muddles too.

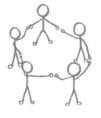

Age group: 5-7, 7-11

Paper butterflies

Make butterflies out of paper and decorate beautifully.

Talk about how bright butterflies come out of a plain cocoon,
and encourage the children to think about something
that they would like to have a new start in too
(for example, playing nicely in the playground,
sharing with brothers and sisters).

Place the butterflies on a flowering tree or plant
to represent the new life that God brings.

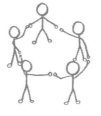

Age group: 5-7, 7-11

God's love door curtain

Cut out hearts from different colour paper, write the words
'God Loves Us' on them and tape them onto long strings or ribbons.

Hang these from a stick cut to the width of the doorway, or fix the
ribbons to the top of the door frame with sticky tack or tape.

As you walk through the door,
think about entering into the love of God.

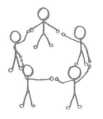

Age group: under 5, 5–7, 7–11

God washes away our sins

Wrap up soap in paper and label with the words:
'God washes away our sins'.

Some soaps can be cut up easily with a wire cheese cutter or knife —
children only need a little piece of soap to wrap and take home.

Talk about how God's forgiveness is like washing all the mud,
sticky food and paint off our hands, so that we can have a new start.

Age group: 5-7, 7-11

whiteboard pen
sorry prayers

Laminate a picture of the world or a map.

First, children can write things that need forgiving in our world.
These can be used in a prayer — for example,
'For the times we fight — forgive us, Lord',
'For the times we are selfish — forgive us, Lord',
'For the times we upset others — forgive us, Lord'.

After this, the children can rub out the words
and replace them with hearts or smiley faces.

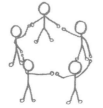

Age group: 7–11

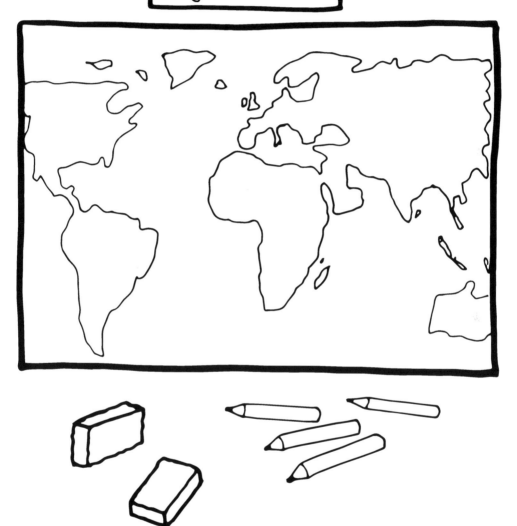

Ice cube hearts

Make ice cubes with small hearts frozen inside.

The hearts can be made from orange peel
(safe for younger children who may put it in their mouths).

Give everyone an ice cube in a cup to melt,
and think of God's love melting our hearts
and helping us to love others.

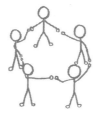

Age group: under 5, 5-7, 7-11

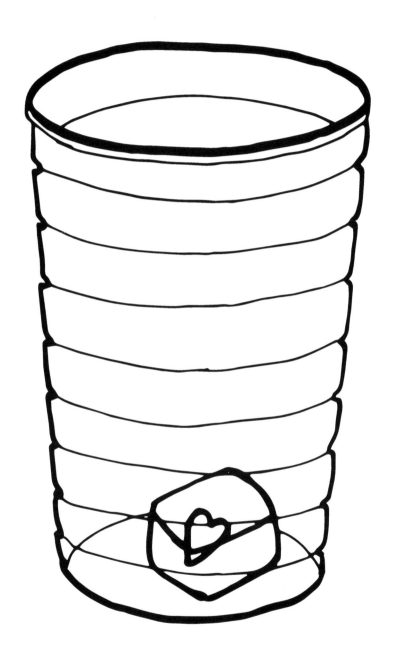

Prayers for other people

Marble-run prayers

A way to think of and pray for others.

The children can set up a marble run and check that it works.
Give each child a marble to hold and ask them to think
of somebody they would like to pray for.

Taking it in turns, they can name the person and set the
marble off on its course. As it rolls down the marble run,
everyone can think of that person and bring them to God.

This provides something for children to focus on
during the prayer, making it a bit more spacious
and showing that each person is special before God.

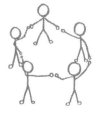

Age group: under 5, 5–7, 7–11

Plaster prayers

Write the names of people who are ill on plasters and
stick the plasters onto a special prayer board, labelled
'Dear God, please bring your love and healing'.

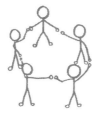

Age group: 5–7, 7–11

Building the kingdom

Using building bricks, make words which are signs of God's kingdom —
for example, peace, love, hope, sharing, listening, helping etc.

Children can work together to make some of the words,
which can then be put in a display.

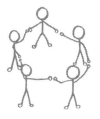

Age group: 5-7, 7-11

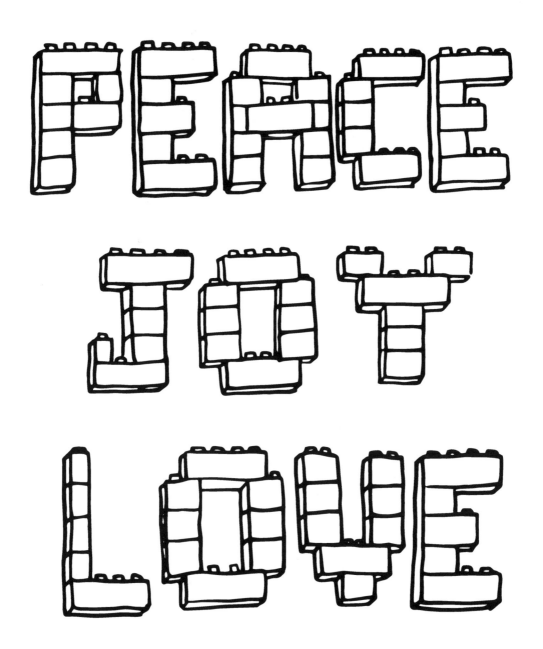

Paper prayer lanterns

Make a paper lantern by folding a piece of A4 paper in half, longways.
Cut slits in it from the middle, stopping 2cms above the edge.
Open the paper up and roll it into a tube shape to form a lantern.
Make a handle out of another strip of paper and write on this:
'Lord, show your light'.

Decorate the lanterns and place them together on a table,
to pray for God's light in situations which seem full of darkness.
If you have some LED tea lights, these can be placed
inside the paper lanterns too.

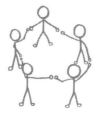

Age group: 5-7, 7-11

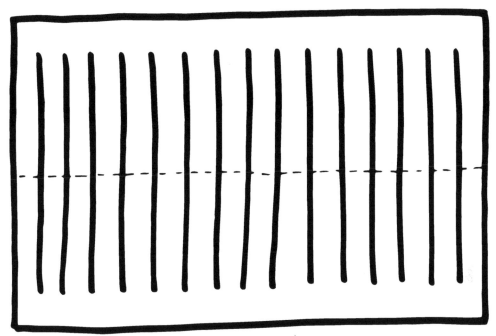

Fold along dotted line, cut slits, then open paper up.

Prayer weaving

Set up a large cardboard loom made from a couple of thicknesses of corrugated card, with zigzags cut into the top and bottom edges and with wool looped around it.

Give children long, thin strips of different coloured fabric or thick paper and ask them to write, using brightly coloured pens, how they would like to help show God's love.

After this, they can weave the strips into the loom.

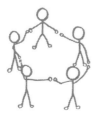

Age group: 5-7, 7-11

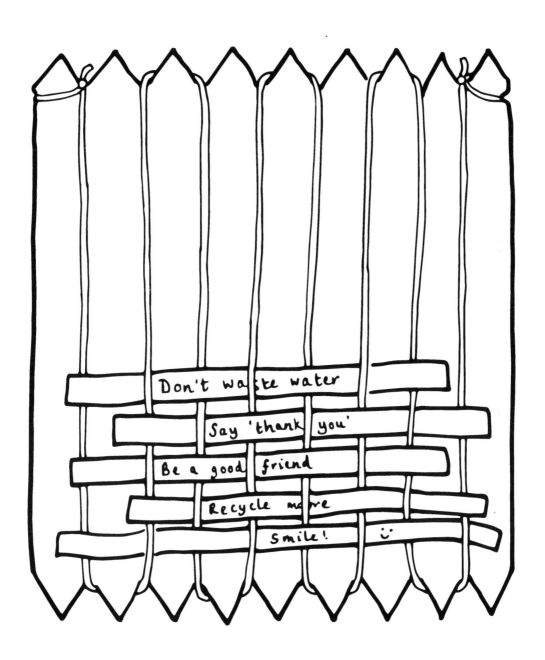

Folded-over card vehicles

These could include emergency vehicles, buses,
cars, lorries, bikes, mobility scooters etc.

Children can colour them in and write a prayer, e.g.
'Look after the people on their scooters',
'Thank you for the paramedics',
'Thank you for the rubbish collectors' etc.

The vehicles can then be lined up on a long paper road.

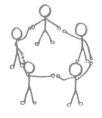

Age group: under 5, 5-7

Bubble prayers

Everyone sits in a circle and thinks of something
or someone that they would like to pray for
(it is fine if people say the same as somebody else).

Pass round the bubble mixture.
After saying a prayer, the children can blow some
bubbles and think of the prayers going up to heaven
as they watch the bubbles floating up to the sky.

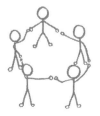

Age group: under 5, 5-7, 7-11

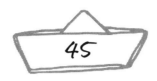

Prayer boats

Make paper boats, draw people on them and maybe some fish,
and float them in a large tray or bowl of water
(or place them on a blue blanket or sheet) while thinking
about and praying for people who work on the sea.

The boats could be decorated to look like a lifeboat,
a fishing boat, a ferry, a sailing boat, a cruise ship etc.

Make a sign saying:
'Dear God, please look after everyone who works on the sea. Amen'.

Age group: 5–7, 7–11

1. Fold an A4 piece of paper in half, then fold the corners in.

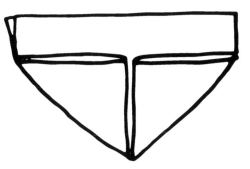

2. Fold the flaps down on the front and the back.

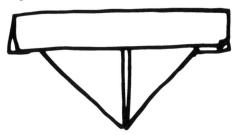

3. Open out, and fold the other way.

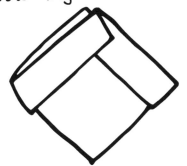

4. Fold the flaps down on both sides.

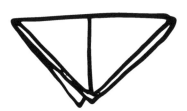

5. Open out, and fold the other way.

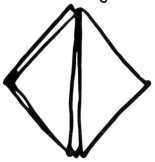

6. Turn it round.

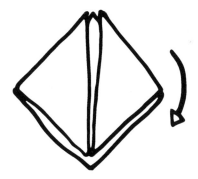

7. Pull out the points from each side.

8. Fold it flat.

Prayer postbox

Children can write a prayer, put it in a real envelope,
decorate it and post it into a cardboard prayer postbox,
remembering that God knows what we are thinking
and can read our prayers straight away.

Younger children can draw pictures and post them.

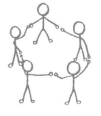

Age group: under 5, 5–7

Prayer hopscotch

Draw a hopscotch pattern with street chalk.

Children first write their own name in one of the squares.
Then they play hopscotch, throwing a stone to a square
and hopping/jumping to that place, thinking of the person
named on the square and bringing them to God.

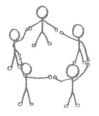

Age group: 5-7, 7-11

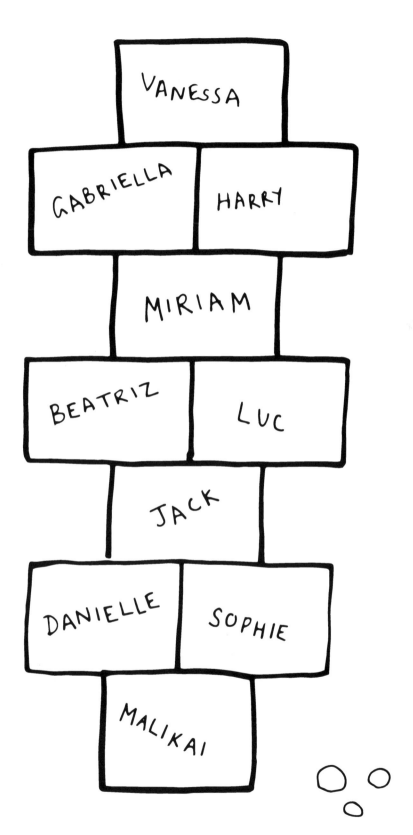

A prayer jigsaw

First cut a large piece of cardboard into jigsaw-shaped pieces.

Then everyone has a piece and draws/writes on it
a way they can help to be a part of God's kingdom.

The jigsaw can then be joined together,
showing how we can all work together.

Age group: 5-7, 7-11

Teapot prayers

Sit in a circle and pass around a plastic teapot
with water in it (labelled 'God gives us living water')
and pour a drink for the person next to you.

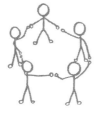

Age group: under 5, 5–7

God gives us living water

Prayer biscuits

Wrap up biscuits in paper, decorate nicely,
write 'God loves you' on it and give it to someone else.

Younger children could be given a piece of paper
to decorate with the words already written on it.

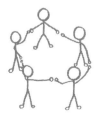

Age group: 5-7, 7-11

Prayer dominoes

This activity matches need and response.

Cut out some blank cardboard dominoes from card and draw a
line across the middle of each of them to divide them into two.

Children can think of areas of need and the solution that we can be
part of. Then they draw these onto the dominoes, so that they match up.

For example, when the dominoes are lined up
the order could be something like this:
Happy face, empty bowl / full bowl, empty cup /
full cup, tent / house, rags / clothes, ill face /
well face with doctor kit, cold person / person with blanket, wilting plants /
healthy plants with watering can, sad face.

This would be a good activity to link up with a charity gift catalogue,
showing practical ways of helping others. Talk about how it's good to pray
for people in need, but that also God can use us to be part of the solution.

Age group: 5-7, 7-11

Prayer bears

Make collage cut-out teddies with felt, tissue paper,
buttons etc. and stick on some words of encouragement,
such as 'God loves you' or 'God is with you'.

Give the bears to someone else.

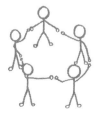

Age group: under 5, 5–7

Prayer percussion

Hang up different objects to ting and bang,
labelled with different areas for prayer
(e.g. those who are ill, friends, family,
the environment, places where there is fighting).

As children bang the objects they can think of
the things they want to bring to God.

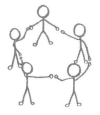

Age group: under 5, 5–7

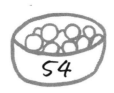

Prayer beads

Have pots with different coloured beads in them
and labelled with different things to pray for.

For example, pink for people you love;
green for forests, trees and plants;
blue for oceans, rivers and seas;
white for the Arctic and Antarctic, glaciers,
mountains and the animals that live there;
red for people who are ill or in pain;
brown to thank God for our food,
and to think of those who don't have enough.

Place the pots around the room and give each child a piece of string,
knotted at one end and wrapped with sticky tape at the other, so that
they can move around the room, prayerfully adding beads as they go.

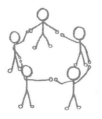

Age group: 5-7, 7-11

PINK
PEOPLE WE LOVE

GREEN
FORESTS AND TREES

WHITE
ARCTIC AND GLACIERS

BLUE
OCEANS, RIVERS + SEAS

RED
PEOPLE WHO ARE ILL

Round the world scrapbook

Save mailings from international development
and mission charities/alternative gift catalogues
(or print them from the internet).

Stick a world map on the front of your scrapbook,
together with the words 'We pray for the world'.

Children can cut out pictures of people from
the catalogues and stick them inside.

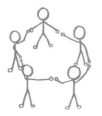

Age group: under 5, 5–7, 7–11

A globe ball

Roll a globe ball (or a plain ball that has had countries
drawn on it with a marker pen or whiteboard pen).

Pray for the country that your finger lands on,
using a simple prayer, such as
'Lord, we pray for Bangladesh – Amen',
'Lord, we pray for Canada – Amen',
'Lord, we pray for Antarctica – Amen',
'Lord, we pray for the Pacific Ocean – Amen'.

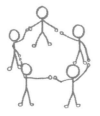

Age group: 5–7, 7–11

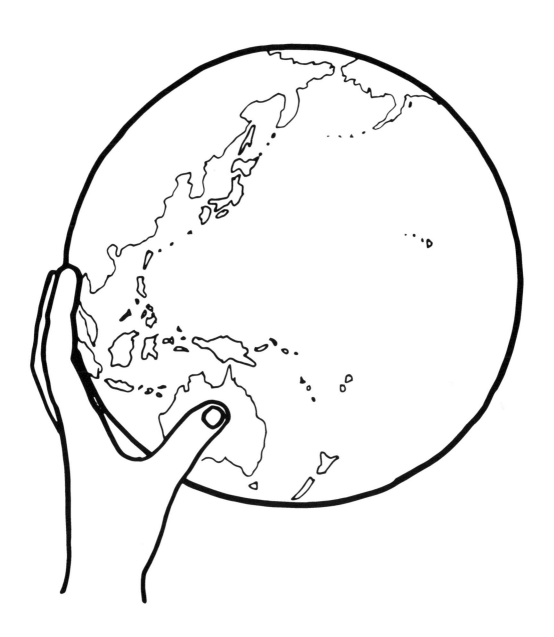

Dove hand prints

These are used as a prayer for peace.

If children hold their little finger and ring finger together to
make a tail, their first finger and middle finger together
to make a wing, and their thumb out to make a head,
this can be printed onto blue card with white paint,
or drawn around to form a dove shape.

Children can add details such as eyes and
a beak to their doves with black pen.

Cut out round the edges of the doves and
stick all the doves onto a poster labelled,
'We pray for peace'.

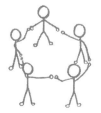

Age group: under 5, 5-7

Prayer globe

Stick Lego® people on a globe with sticky tack,
to help pray for people around the world.

Sit in a circle with the globe in the middle and sing
'He's got the whole world in his hands'.

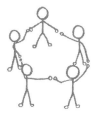

Age group: under 5, 5–7, 7–11

Magnetic fishing prayers

Draw and cut out sea creatures from paper and put
a small paper clip on the nose of each of them.

Make fishing rods from sticks and string, with a magnet tied on
(a magnetic letter is usually easy to find, and easy to tie on,
and will pick up the paper creatures if they are not too big).

Children can sit in a circle and take it in turns to fish for an animal.

When they find one, say a prayer such as:
'Help us to look after the seals — Amen',
'Help us look after the sharks — Amen',
'Help us look after the dolphins — Amen'.

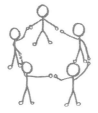

Age group: under 5, 5–7

Magnetic letter prayers

Write on a magnetic whiteboard the words
'We pray for . . .',
and children can use magnetic letters
to add words underneath.

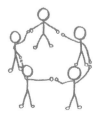

Age group: 5–7, 7–11

Prayer conkers

Draw a heart or smiley face on a conker.

Everyone holds their conker in their hand.
Sit in a circle and sing 'He's got the whole world in his hands',
thinking about how God cares for our world and loves us.

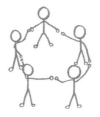

Age group: under 5, 5–7

Big knitting/finger knitting

This is used to 'yarn bomb' and show the warmth of God's love.

By winding some wool in between the fingers of one hand
to make four rows, it is possible to loop the wool over
itself to create a length of loose, soft knitting.

This can then be wrapped around objects such as chairs,
tables and pillars, with a luggage tag style label which says
'God loves you'.

Age group: 7-11

1.

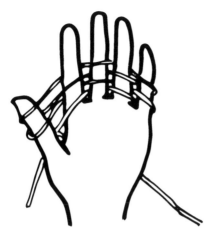

Wind wool in and out of fingers.

2.

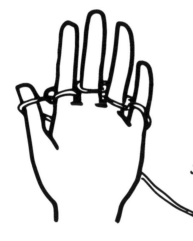

Lift the lower loop over the top of each finger, so it starts to form loose knitting at the back.

3.

Wind the wool round your fingers again, and repeat step 2.

water obstacle race

Divide the children into equal-sized teams.

Each team has a full bucket of water near the start of the race,
an empty bottle of water at the end of the race and a plastic cup.

Set up some obstacles to climb over and under
(chairs, tables, benches etc.).

The children have to take it in turns to carry water in the cup
through all the obstacles to fill the bucket at the end of the race.

The first team to fill their bucket is the winner.

Label the bucket at the start with the words
'Thank you, God, for water',
and the bucket at the end with the words
'We pray for people who don't have clean water'.

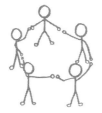

Age group: under 5, 5–7

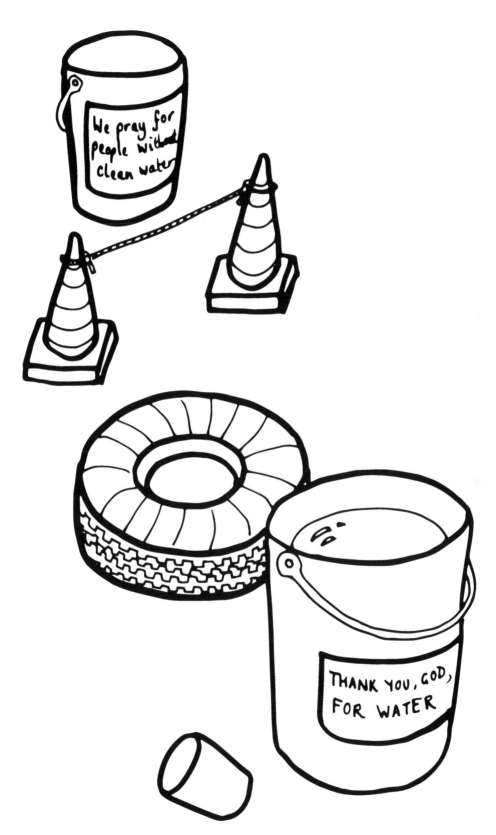

Milk bottle lid faces

Everyone draws their face on a milk bottle lid
and writes their name on it.

Put the lids together in a tub or bag and ask children to
pick someone else's lid, take it home and pray for them.

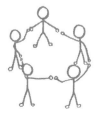

Age group: under 5, 5-7, 7-11

65

Prayer map

Make a map of your community,
with the surrounding roads, trees, open spaces,
shops, schools, and other buildings marked on it.

Give each child some heart stickers
(or paper hearts with sticky tack on the back)
to stick onto the map as a prayer for that place.

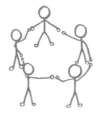

Age group: 5-7, 7-11

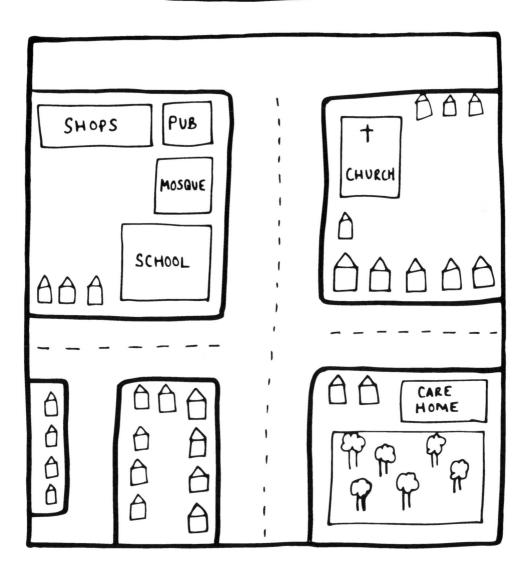

SHOPS PUB

MOSQUE

SCHOOL

CHURCH

CARE HOME

A papier-mâché dove

Cut out a dove shape from corrugated card
and children can use flour and water paste to
stick strips of newspaper onto it, covering the dove.

Talk about how the dove is a symbol of peace
and how we can pray to God to bring peace in
the situations we see in the news.

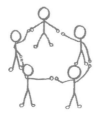

Age group: 5-7, 7-11

Days of the week prayer themes

Cut out two same-sized circles of card and cut a window in one of them.

Join the two pieces of card together with a split pin, with the window card on top. Write the names of the days of the week through the window, turning the top wheel a little each time.

Go back round again, adding themes for each day — for example,
Sunday — pray for the church and its leaders;
Monday — pray for our friends;
Tuesday — pray for our families;
Wednesday — pray for people we find it hard to get along with;
Thursday — pray for everyone who is ill;
Friday — pray for our world and the environment;
Saturday — pray for world leaders.

Children could shade the background of each section a different colour and decorate the front of the prayer wheel.

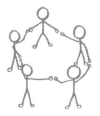

Age group: 5–7, 7–11

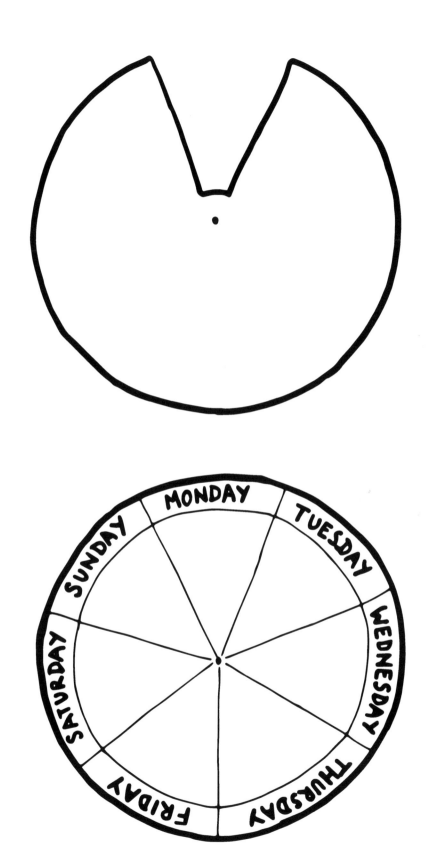

Beanbag prayers

Draw buildings and places on the floor with street chalk,
or mark them on a large piece of paper with a pen.

These could include a hospital, school, church, shop, park etc.
Children can take it in turns to throw a beanbag onto a building
and pray for all the people who are in that place.

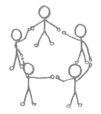

Age group: under 5, 5–7

Blessings written in invisible pen

The children each write a blessing using an invisible pen,
then swap with someone else and read the blessing with UV light
(it is possible to buy on the internet multiple packs of invisible pens,
with UV lights on the end, for party bags and groups).

Words could include things like
'God loves you',
'God bless you',
'God is with you', and
'Talk to God, he loves to listen to you'.

Age group: 5-7, 7-11

A prayer 'chatterbox' or 'colour changer'

These are made by folding paper, with different colours on the outside, then numbers inside, and prayers written underneath the flaps.

For example: outside — green, blue, yellow, or red (count the letters and open and shut the chatterbox that number of times). Inside — different numbers (open and shut the chatterbox that number of times). Under the flaps — 'We pray for the beautiful world that we share. Help us all, Lord, to treat it with care. Amen'; 'We pray for the people fleeing from war. Bring peace and love back to their countries once more. Amen'; 'Look after our aunties and sisters and mothers, our fathers and uncles and cousins and brothers. Amen'; 'We pray for the people who are ill or in pain. Please bring them your healing and love once again. Amen'.

Younger children could just do the folding part of the activity, if a finished chatterbox is opened out, dotted lines added to show where to fold, photocopied and trimmed back into a square shape.

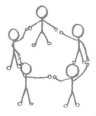

Age group: 5–7, 7–11

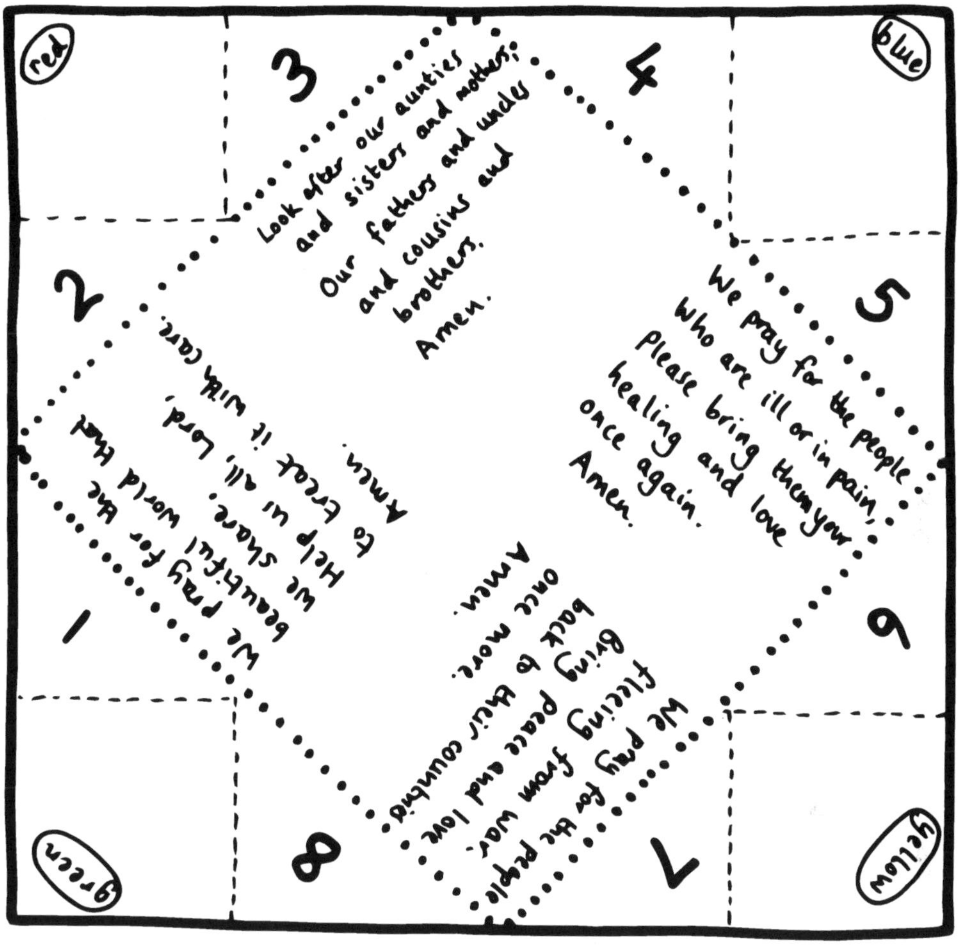
red
blue
green
yellow
1
2
3
4
5
6
7
8
Look after our aunties and sisters and mothers; Our fathers and uncles and cousins and brothers. Amen.
We pray for the people Who are ill or in pain, Please bring them your healing and love once again. Amen.
We pray for the people fleeing from war. Bring peace and love back to their countries once more. Amen.
We pray for the beautiful world that we share. Help us all, Lord, to treat it with care. Amen.

······· fold first

- - - - - fold second

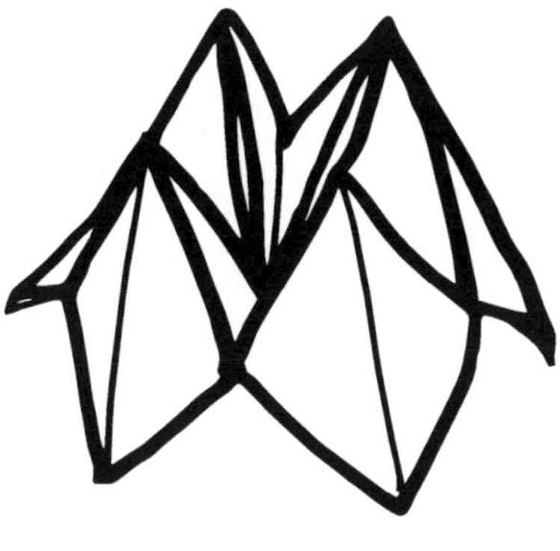

A prayer tree

Add paper leaves with prayers on to a cardboard tree
with names of people or things to pray for.

This could be a way of praying for others
in a church, group, or school class.

Everyone writes another person's name on a leaf
and adds it to the tree as a prayer for them.

Age group: 5-7, 7-11

72

Prayer lolly sticks

Children have a lolly stick each and write a short prayer
of encouragement on it in ballpoint pen – for example,
'Be strong',
'God loves you',
'You are special',
'You are precious',
'God cares about you', or
'You are part of God's family'.

Place the lolly sticks in a tray of sand,
so that the messages are hidden.

Everyone can pick a different lolly stick
and take the blessing home with them.

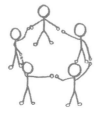

Age group: 5–7, 7–11

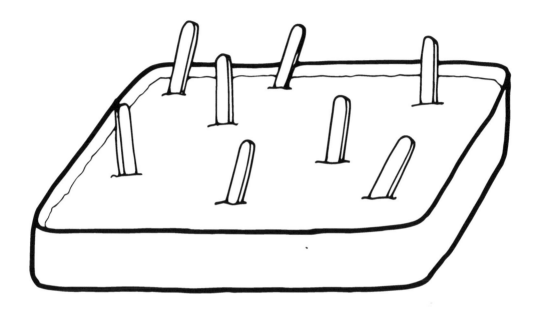

Prayers for ourselves

Iced biscuits

Decorate iced biscuits with raisins and different coloured sweets from pots labelled with characteristics we would like God to help us with (e.g. patience, kindness, persistence, sharing, generosity, love, understanding etc.).

Older children could help to come up with ideas for the labels for the pots.

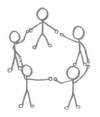

Age group: under 5, 5-7, 7-11

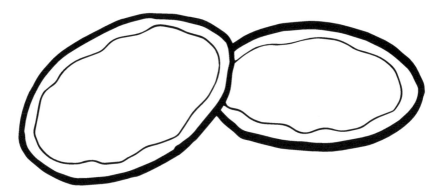

Cardboard hearts

Cut out cardboard hearts in various colours.

Children write 'God Loves' on them and stick
on a photo of themselves (or draw a picture)
and write their name underneath.

Punch a hole in the cardboard and
hang up the hearts with string or wool.

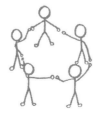

Age group: under 5, 5-7

Plant a mini prayer garden

Children could plant a plug plant each and
put a lolly stick with their name on next to it.

Have a sign up saying
'We plant ourselves in your love, Lord'.

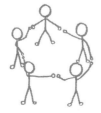

Age group: under 5, 5–7

Paper dolls

Dress a paper doll with a breastplate of righteousness,
helmet of salvation, shoes of the Gospel of Peace,
sword of the Spirit, belt of truth and shield of faith.

If you draw the outline of a person first, this can be used
to trace the shapes of the clothes so that they fit.

Children can cut the items out of paper, with flaps
left on so that they can fold them around
the paper dolls and colour them in.

Talk about how God gives us the things we need
to live the right way for him, and we can imagine
putting them on like clothes in the morning.

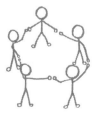

Age group: 5–7, 7–11

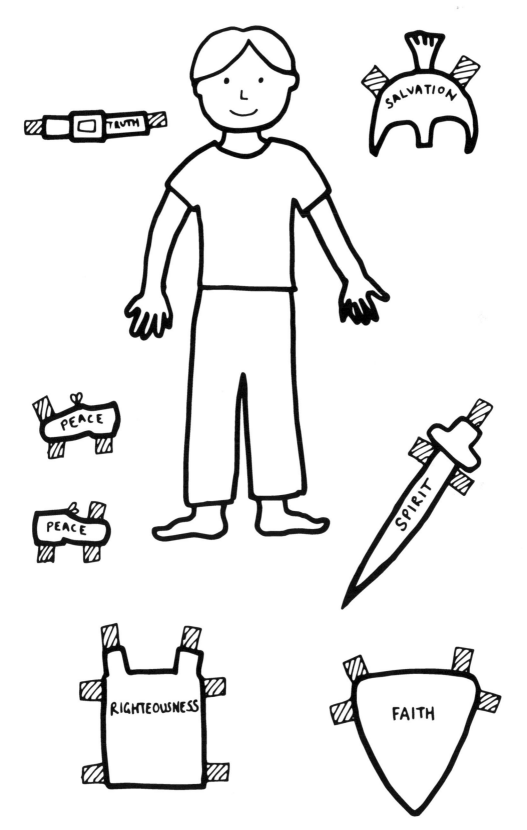

Seed cups

Label/decorate a paper cup with the words
'We are growing in your love',
fill it with soil and plant seeds in it.

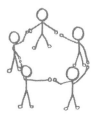

Age group: under 5, 5-7, 7-11

78

Invisible messages

Write with white wax crayon or candles on paper:
'Show us your ways, Lord'
and paint over this using watercolours.
The message will show up.

Younger children could be helped to draw
a heart shape, to represent God's love.

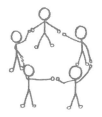

Age group: under 5, 5-7, 7-11

79

God's blessings mocktails

Fill jugs with different fruit juices, labelled with
qualities we would like God to help us with
(e.g. faith, humility, compassion, patience, strength).

Children can mix and match, thinking of God
filling them up as they fill their cups.

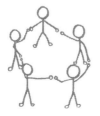

Age group: under 5, 5-7, 7-11

Prayer compasses

Make a compass (real or pretend) and label it with the words, 'Jesus, show us the way'.

A pretend compass can be made by cutting out a circle of card and an arrow, joining them together with a split pin, and labelling the directions N, S, E and W.

A real compass can be made by stroking a needle with a magnet, always in one direction, to magnetise it.

The needle can then be fixed onto a plastic bottle lid with sticky tack, and placed in a small bowl of water so that it is floating.

The compass will rotate around until the needle is pointing N/S.

Age group: 5–7, 7–11

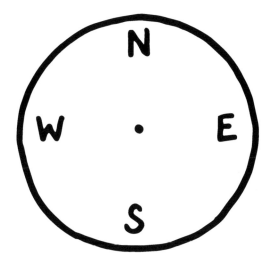

Cardboard compass with
split pin

Working compass with
magnetised needle

Fruit bags

Fill food bags with different cut-up
pieces of fruit, set out on plates which
are labelled with the fruits of the Spirit
(love, joy, peace, patience, kindness, goodness,
faithfulness, gentleness and self-control).

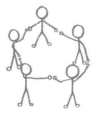

Age group: 5-7, 7-11

Prayer feet

Draw round feet,
cut them out and write the words
'We are following Jesus' on them,
then stick them on a paper path.

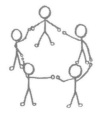

Age group: under 5, 5–7

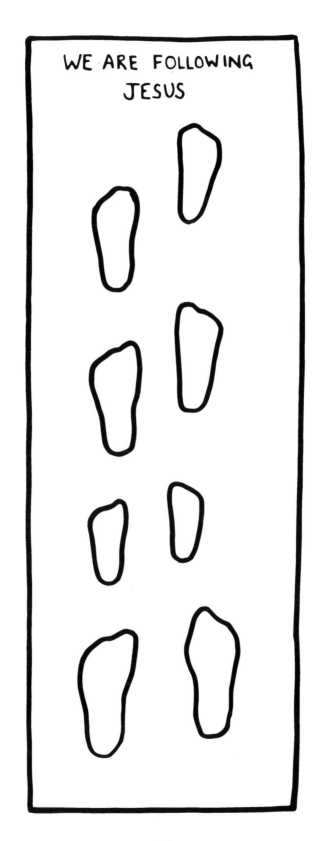

83

Sunflowers

Grow sunflowers in pots labelled
'We are reaching up to God's light'.

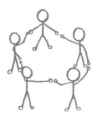

Age group: under 5, 5-7, 7-11

Milkshake bar

Fill large jugs with milkshakes
(milk whisked up with ice-cream, jam or mashed fruit).

Label them with signs such as:
caring chocolate, saintly strawberry,
blessed banana, prayerful/peaceful peach,
loving loganberry and meaningful mint.

Children can think about how they can receive
God's blessings and strength while they enjoy choosing,
pouring and drinking the milkshakes.

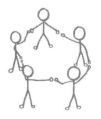

Age group: under 5, 5–7, 7–11

A cardboard box church

Make a cardboard box church,
ask everyone to draw their face on a
sticky label and place it on the church.

Label the box with the words
'We are the Church — please bless us as we worship God together'.

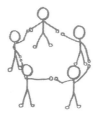

Age group: under 5, 5-7, 7-11

WE ARE THE CHURCH—
PLEASE BLESS US
AS WE WORSHIP GOD
TOGETHER

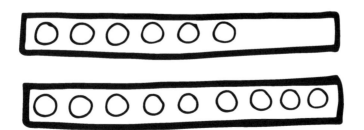

86

A playground/outdoor prayer path

Draw a path or labyrinth outside.

Write these words along the path, so that
children can read them as they walk or run along:
'Be with us, Lord, on our journey through life'.

Older children can research and draw different labyrinth designs.

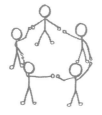

Age group: under 5, 5–7, 7–11

Height chart

Make a height chart out of long strips of paper,
marked with centimetres and metres.

Write these words at the side:
'Be with us as we grow, Lord'.

Age group: under 5, 5–7

Bubble writing

Everyone writes their own name in bubble writing
and fills it in with colours that are labelled
to represent God's blessings and promises
(blue for peace, orange for wisdom,
yellow for joy, green for growth,
purple for prayer, red for strength,
pink for love).

Children can choose the colours and
blessings that appeal to them.

Younger children could be given their name
already written in bubble writing and
could concentrate on colouring it in.

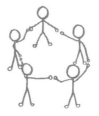

Age group: under 5, 5-7, 7-11

Things to remind us to pray

A prayer clock

Make a cardboard clock as a reminder to pray at all times of the day.
You will need: card, scissors, pens, a split pin, some ribbon and
something round to use as a template, such as a saucer.

First, draw and cut out a circle from the card. Younger children
could be given card with a circle already drawn on it.

Write the words 'Pray round the clock' round the edge of the circle,
and then write the numbers 1–12 to make the clock face.

Cut out two hands for the clock and fix them to the middle of the clock
face with the split pin (children might need some adult help with this).

Explain to the children that we can talk to God at
any time of the day and he is always ready to listen.

Age group: 5–7, 7–11

90

Bedtime prayers 'lucky dip'

Make a 'lucky dip' to put in an envelope and take home.

These could include traditional bedtime prayers
and also perhaps some new ones, such as these:

'Thank you, God, for our cosy beds,
a lovely place to rest our heads';
'Dear God, I'm sleepy now, but I wanted to say,
thank you for being with me today';
'Dear Lord, please help me grow and help me rest,
and help me try to do my best'.

Children could be given the photocopied prayers to colour
and decorate, or could copy them onto plain paper.

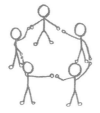

Age group: under 5, 5–7

Thank you, God,
for our cosy beds,
a lovely place
to rest our heads.
Amen.

☆ Dear God, ☆
I'm sleepy now,
but I wanted to say,
☆ thank you for being
with me today.
☆ Amen.

Dear God,
Please help me grow,
and help me rest,
and help me try
to do my best.
Amen.

97

A prayer wheel

Make a prayer wheel from three circles of cardboard
and a split pin — line up the combinations you
choose to make an outline for prayer.

The outside wheel could have words or pictures of
things to be thankful for, the next wheel could
have different people or situations to pray for,
and the inside wheel could have things to ask for ourselves.

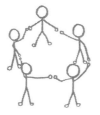

Age group: 5-7, 7-11

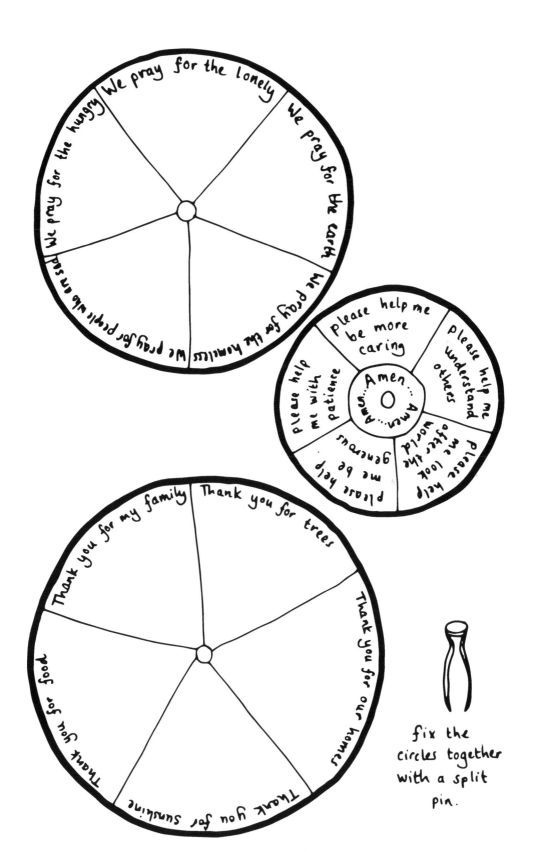

We pray for the lonely

We pray for the hungry

We pray for the earth

We pray for the families

We pray for people who are sad

please help me be more caring

please help me understand others

please help me look after the world

please help me be generous

please help me with patience

Amen Amen Amen Amen

Thank you for my family

Thank you for trees

Thank you for our homes

Thank you for sunshine

Thank you for food

fix the circles together with a split pin.

92

Prayer puppets

Make simple puppets with socks and stickers.

Children can use the puppets to help them say prayers
out loud, perhaps when sitting in a circle and passing
round a prayer book or box of prayer cards.

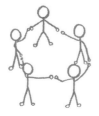

Age group: under 5, 5-7

93

Easter crosses

Make Easter crosses out of natural materials
such as sticks, grass, flowers, blossom,
leaves, feathers, shells and bark.

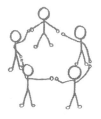

Age group: under 5, 5-7, 7-11

94

A prayer bracelet

Make a plaited bracelet from three long
different coloured strands of wool,
doubled over and a loop tied in the end.

Stick the looped end down onto a table or knee
with some tape, to keep it still, and separate
the wool into double strands of matching colours.

Plait the wool together and then tie a knot in the end.

Children can wear the three stranded bracelets
to remind them that God is with them,
Father, Son and Holy Spirit.

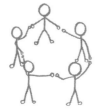

Age group: 5-7, 7-11

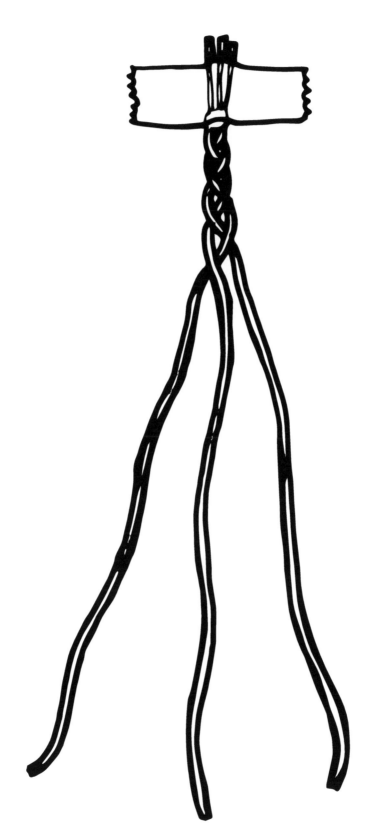

A sewing card cross

Make a sewing card cross with holes punched round
the edge and wool to thread through the holes.
Wind some tape around one end of the wool
(to make it more rigid for threading)
and tie a knot in the other end
(or tie it onto the first sewing hole).

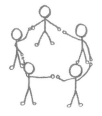

Age group: under 5, 5-7

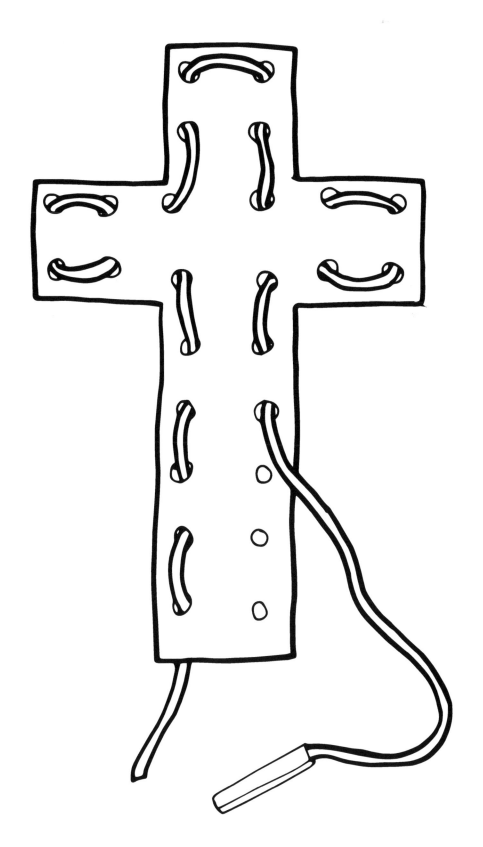

Toast crosses

Press a cross shape into a slice of bread with a
teaspoon, toast the bread and the shape will show up.

This could be a reminder to pray as we eat,
or to use as an activity on Good Friday.

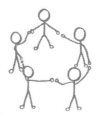

Age group: under 5, 5-7, 7-11

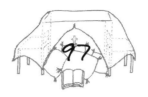

A prayer den

Make a prayer den out of chairs, tables, blankets and
sheets, held on with strong elastic bands and clothes pegs.

Put a cushion, a cross, prayer beads and
a prayer book or prayer cards inside,
and children can go in one or two at a time to pray.

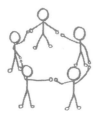

Age group: under 5, 5–7

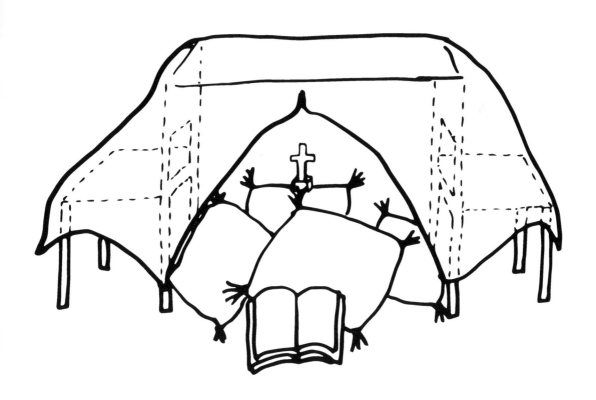

98

Pipe cleaner cross pencil toppers

Make a pipe cleaner cross pencil topper
by folding a pipe cleaner in half,
pinching out the sides to make a cross shape
and then winding the ends around a pencil.

The cross can be held in place with sticky tape.

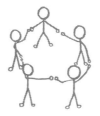

Age group: 5-7, 7-11

99

A pompom rug

Make a pompom rug for a prayer corner.

This is a good way of using up anyone's spare wool, as any
colours or thicknesses are fine. Everyone makes a pompom,
by winding wool around a bottle, tin or hand (not too tightly!).

The looped wool can be tied together with a
shorter piece and the loops cut with scissors.

These pompoms can be attached to some backing
fabric by threading the knotted wool through
with a needle and tying it securely at the back.

If lots of people are helping to make the pompoms,
a rug can be made very quickly.

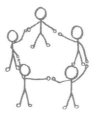

Age group: 5-7, 7-11

A prayer spinner

Make a spinner from a hexagon of cardboard,
with a pencil through the middle.

In each section of the hexagon, write a short prayer –
'Thank you for our friends',
'Thank you for the world',
'Thank you for our homes',
'Look after people who are ill',
'Thank you for our food',
'Be with people who are sad'.

In the middle of the hexagon, write the words:
'Dear God . . . Amen . . .'
to provide the beginning and end of the prayers.

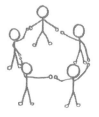

Age group: 5–7, 7–11

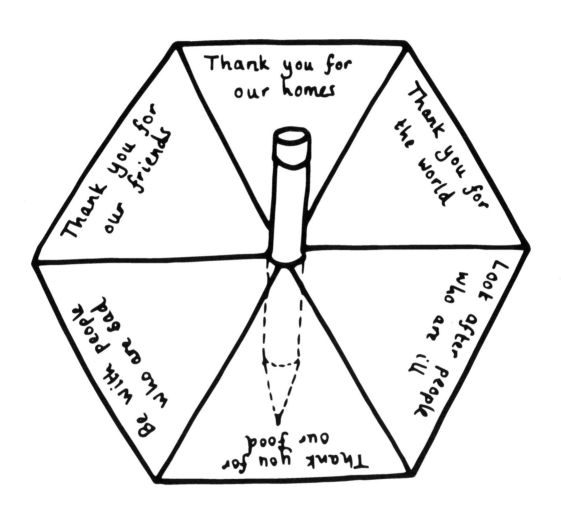

The Lord's Prayer

The Lord's Prayer is written in a spiral and cut out —
this can be hung up with a piece of wool or string.

Younger children can be given a photocopied version with
the words already on it, for them to colour and cut out.

Age group: 5-7, 7-11

cut around spiral

Our Father, who art in heaven, hallowed be thy name. Thy kingdom come, Thy will be done, on earth as it is in heaven. Give us this day our daily bread, and forgive us our trespasses, as we forgive those who trespass against us. And lead us not into temptation, but deliver us from evil. For thine is the kingdom, the power and the glory, forever and ever. Amen.